WISDOM
THE MIDWAY ALBATROSS

Darcy Pattison

Kitty Harvill

Surviving the Japanese Tsunami and other Disasters for over 60 Years

mims

Wisdom, the Midway Albatross:
Surviving the Japanese Tsunami
and other Disasters for over 60 Years

JNF003270 JUVENILE NONFICTION / Animals /
　 Endangered
JNF003030 JUVENILE NONFICTION / Animals /
　 Birds

EPub: ISBN 9780979862182
Paperback: ISBN 9780979862175

http://albatross.darcypattison.com

Mims House
1309 S. Broadway
Little Rock, AR 72202
USA

Kitty Harvill
Dedicated to albatrosses and seabirds everywhere.

Darcy Pattison
For my grandchildren and their grandchildren.

Acknowledgments
Thanks to Pete Leary, Wildlife Biologist, Midway Atoll
National Wildlife Refuge, Papahānaumokuākea Marine
National Monument for his help in this project and for his
excellent photography, which is the basis for much of the
watercolors here. We also thank these photographers for the
use of their work as reference material: John Klavitter, David
Patte, Brenda Zuan, and Michael Lusk.

Many years ago, on the tiny Midway Atoll in the heart of the Pacific Ocean, a wild chick hatched. She was a gooney bird—a Laysan Albatross. The crowded, noisy rookery could be a dangerous place. Many chicks would not live long enough to learn to fly.

Somehow, Gooney survived.

When it was time to migrate, Gooney was
gone for a long time. For five or six or
seven or eight years, she soared.
When she was hungry, she swooped down
to land on the waves to eat.
She liked squid best, but she wasn't picky.
And always while eating,
she watched the water because sharks liked
to eat goonies.

Somehow, Gooney survived.

One day in 1952, while Gooney
was still a youngster soaring
over the open ocean,
an earthquake hit Kamchatka,
Russia and a tsunami
sped across the Pacific Ocean,
to crash against the shores of
Midway Atoll and Hawaii.
If she noticed the huge wave,
it didn't bother her.

Gooney just flew
above the tsunami.
This time, it was easy to survive.

Finally, after years of soaring,
Gooney flew south
in search of love.
In about 1956,
she landed back
on Midway Atoll.

There, in a noisy courtship dance, she mated.

Soon after, Gooney laid an egg.
She didn't squawk or call. She just sat.
Nothing could make her move
off the nest until her mate
came back from fishing.
She didn't move
for Navy men
who sailed in
submarines or
flew in airplanes.
She didn't move
for airplanes
or trucks
or carts.
She just
sat.

That's when a research scientist, Chandler Robbins, caught her and banded her on December 10, 1956. If she was caught again, the metal leg band would identify her for scientific study.

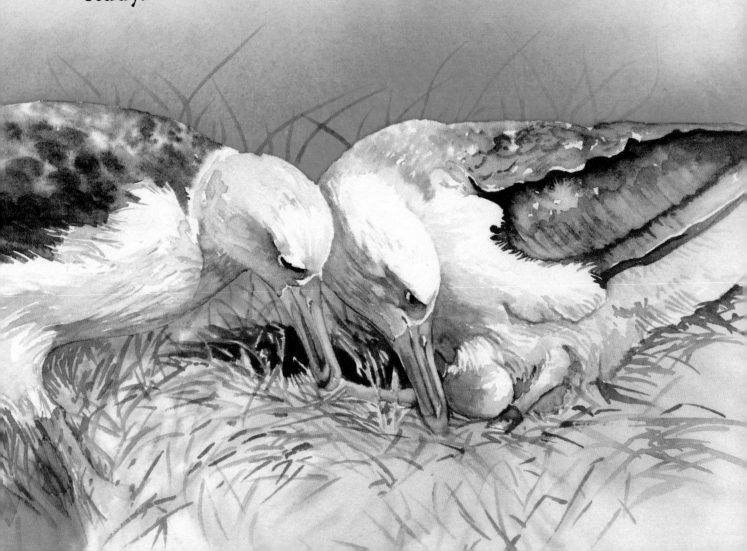

Gooney didn't care about the metal band
on her leg. Soon, she and her mate were too busy
soaring out to sea and coming back to regurgitate
squid to feed the chick.
Finally, when the weather
grew warm, the family flew north.

Gooney and her mate ate and migrated and soared
and raised a new chick each year or so. Thunder-
storms came and went.
Tropical storms came and went.
Hurricanes came and went.
Every year,
more of Gooney's rookery mates
were gone, lost to the wild.
By the time she was
twenty, she had outlived
eighty-seven percent of her rookery mates.

Somehow, Gooney survived.

Eating was always dangerous
for Gooney, but by the 1960s,
it became even more dangerous.
Sitting on the waves and fishing, many
Laysan Albatrosses
started to eat plastic.

Some ate plastic and ate plastic
and ate plastic until
their stomachs were so full
that no food would fit:
                    they starved to death.

Somehow, Gooney survived.

Then, another danger threatened Gooney
and her family, longline fishing.
On a longline, up to 2500
hand-baited hooks are tied
to fishing lines several miles long.
Many Laysan Albatrosses were caught
in the lines and died.

Somehow, Gooney survived.

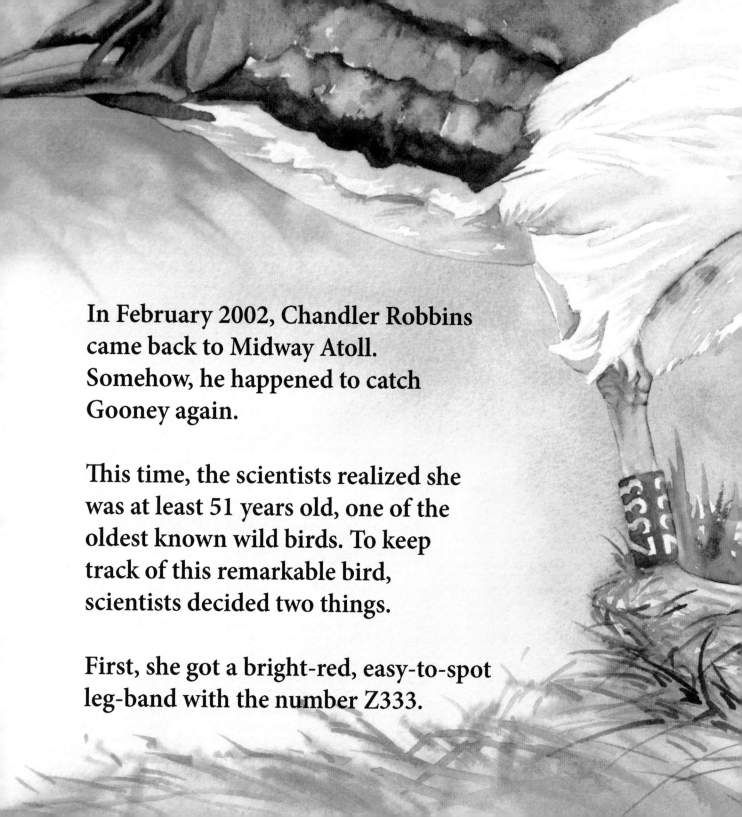

In February 2002, Chandler Robbins came back to Midway Atoll. Somehow, he happened to catch Gooney again.

This time, the scientists realized she was at least 51 years old, one of the oldest known wild birds. To keep track of this remarkable bird, scientists decided two things.

First, she got a bright-red, easy-to-spot leg-band with the number Z333.

Second, she got a name:
Wisdom.

Wisdom, the gooney bird,
returned to lay an egg and
hatch a new baby chick
in 2008, in 2009, and in 2010.

In 2011, Wisdom laid yet another egg,
maybe her 35th. Everyone wondered,
would this chick live as long as
Wisdom?

The chick hatched in February.
A winter storm hit soon after with a
big storm surge, washing across the
island and destroying
about 10,000 chicks.

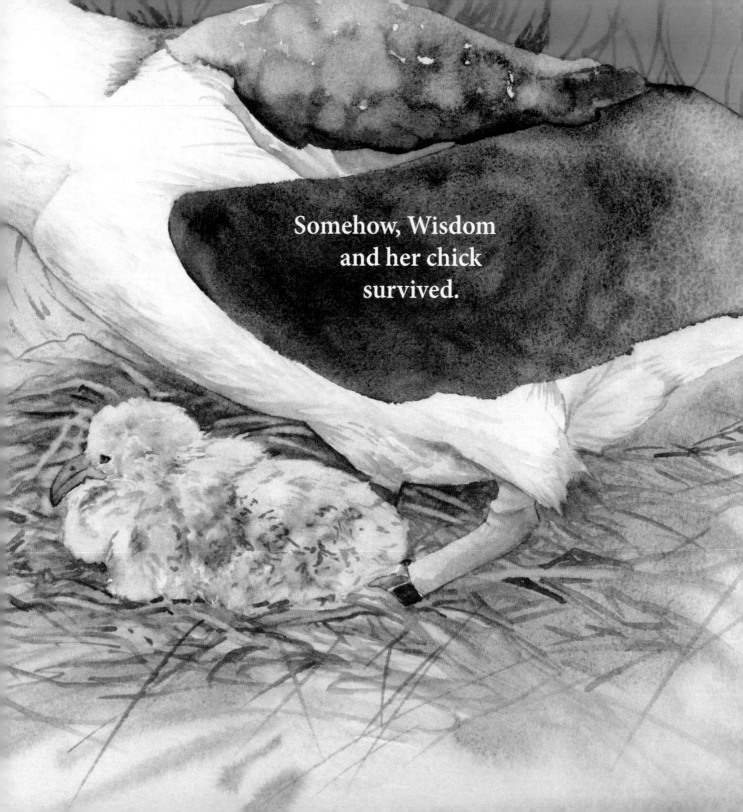

Somehow, Wisdom
and her chick
survived.

Then, on March 11, 2011,
an earthquake struck off the shore of Japan.

It sent a tsunami wave west to overrun Tōhoku, Japan, destroying entire cities, killing thousands of people and damaging a nuclear plant. But the wave also traveled east toward Midway Atoll. Scientists knew the tsunami was coming, so they moved to the top of a three-story building. About midnight, on March 11, the tsunami overran part of Midway Atoll. The scientists said it was scary because they couldn't see the water coming, they just heard it. All the scientists survived. But everyone wondered about the nesting birds. Wisdom's nest was on high ground, but was it high enough? No one knew.

The morning sun showed the
devastation: many birds were dead,
including 110,000 chicks and over 2000
adult Laysan Albatrosses.

Where was Wisdom?
Where was her chick?

When they finally had time
to look, good news!
Wisdom's nest had survived!
The chick was safe.
But where was Wisdom?

No one knew.

Everyone waited.
A week went by. Still no Wisdom.
Eight days. No Wisdom.
Nine days. No Wisdom.
Finally, on March 20, the answer came:
scientists spotted Wisdom
feeding her chick.

Somehow, Wisdom had survived.
Again.

For over sixty years, Wisdom had been
threatened by storms and wind and
sharks and plastic and longline
fishing and earthquakes and
tsunamis. All that time, Wisdom had
lived wild, soaring over the heart
of the great blue ocean and
raising dozens of chicks.

For over sixty years
—somehow—
Wisdom survived.

FACTS ABOUT WISDOM

Laysan Albatross, *Phoebastria immutabilis*

The Laysan Albatross is best known for its gliding flight, awkward landings, and elaborate courtship rituals. These birds spend nearly half the year at sea, not touching land until breeding season. Though large for a seabird, the Laysan is small for an albatross. We don't know the average lifespan of Laysans, but Wisdom is over 60 years old. These birds are named for Laysan, one of their Hawaiian island breeding colonies.

Born: Unknown, presumed Midway Atoll, c. 1950.
Weight: about 8 lbs.
Wingspan: about 6 ½ feet (77-80 inches, or about 2 meters)

THE OLDEST BIRD IN THE WORLD

Wisdom's age has been documented with metal bands on her leg.

DECEMBER 10, 1956 First banded by Chandler Robbins; bird was presumed to be five years old, the minimum age for first breeding.

JANUARY 20, 1966 Second banding by Chandler Robbins.

FEBRUARY 18, 1985 Third banding.

MARCH 4, 1993 Fourth banding.

FEBRUARY 2002 Fifth banding by Chandler Robbins.

DECEMBER 6, 2006 Two new bandings (#6 & #7). This time, Wisdom received a new metal band and a bright red band, Z333; and she was given the name *Wisdom* by former Refuge Biologist, and current Deputy Refuge Manager, John Klavitter.

TYPICAL YEAR FOR A LAYSAN ALBATROSS

October - In late October, the first Laysan Albatrosses return to nesting sites.
November - Most have returned; by late November, some eggs are laid.
December - Most eggs are laid this month.
January - Late January, Laysan Albatross chicks start to hatch.
February - By the end of month, all chicks have hatched.
March - Chicks are starting to wander from the nest.
April - Chicks continue to grow and become more adventurous.
May - Chicks show some adult feathers.
June - Chicks are almost full grown; some adults are leaving the island.
July - More juvenile Laysan Albatrosses are fledging,
and only a few adults remain in the nesting area.
August - By early August, all juvenile Laysan Albatross have flown to sea.
September - No Laysan Albatrosses are left on the island.

Read more

Wisdom A. Laysan Albatross Facebook page, run by the US Fish and
Wildlife Service: www.facebook.com/WisdomtheAlbatross
Save the Albatross: A Global Campaign by BirdLife International
http://www.rspb.org.uk/supporting/campaigns/albatross/
Bird Banding
North American Bird Banding Laboratory:
http://www.pwrc.usgs.gov/bbl/
Global banding: http://www.pwrc.usgs.gov/bbl/manual/birdobs.cfm
Tsunamis: www.tsunami.noaa.gov
Plastic pollution: http://plasticpollutioncoalition.org/
or http://5gyres.org

KITTY HARVILL

www.facebook.com/KittyHarvill

Kitty Harvill specializes in wildlife art, especially endangered species, and works in watercolor, pastel, oil and cut-paper. She has a dual residency in the Arkansas/U.S. and Brazil and is actively involved with the conservation efforts in southern Brazil. Recent titles include *Up! Up! Up! It's Apple-Picking Time* (Holiday House) and *Vida Livre*, with Brazilian author Adélia Woellner , a story about the endangered Red-tailed parrot. Born in Clarksville, Tennessee, Harvill holds a BFA cum laude in painting from SMU and an MA in art therapy from the University of Illinois at Chicago, and an AA in illustration from Ray College, Chicago.

DARCY PATTISON

www.DarcyPattison.com

Published in eight languages, Darcy Pattison's recent children's nature books include *Prairie Storms* (Sylvan Dell) and the forthcoming *Desert Baths* (Sylvan Dell). Her books have been recognized for excellence by starred reviews in Kirkus and BCCB, Child magazine and Nick Jr. Family Magazine Best Books of the Year lists and various state reading award lists. She was the 2007 recipient of the Arkansas Governor's Arts Awards, Individual Artist Award for her work in children's literature. Darcy and her husband have three daughters, one son, three sons-in-law, one granddaughter and two grandsons. When not writing, she can be found quilting or hiking.